SCALING AND MANAGING GROWTH FOR MOBILE APPS 101

Table Of Contents

Chapter 1: Recognizing the Need to Scale

- Indicators of Scalability Needs
- Proactive vs. Reactive Scaling

Chapter 2: Infrastructure Scaling - Vertical vs. Horizontal

- The Benefits and Limitations of Vertical Scaling
- Advantages of Horizontal Scaling and Distribution

Chapter 3: Optimizing App Architecture for Scalability

- Stateless Design Principles for Scalable Apps
- Database Optimization Techniques

Chapter 4: Cloud Solutions for App Growth

- Embracing Cloud Platforms for Flexible Scaling
- Auto-Scaling and Global Distribution Features

Chapter 5: Monitoring, Analytics, and Understanding User Behavior

- Essential Tools for Performance Monitoring
- Analyzing User Patterns for Proactive Scaling

Chapter 6: The Role of Content Delivery Networks (CDNs)

- Introduction to CDNs and Their Benefits
- Implementing CDNs for Mobile App Growth

Chapter 7: Load Balancing and Distributed Systems

- The Mechanics of Load Balancing in Scalable Systems
- Exploring Modern Distributed System Architectures

Chapter 8: Ensuring Data Integrity and Security During Scaling

- Addressing Data Consistency Challenges
- Security Protocols for Growing Mobile Apps

Chapter 9: Continuous Integration and Continuous Deployment (CI/CD)

- Streamlining Development with CI Pipelines
- Best Practices in CD for Scaling Apps

INTRODUCTION: THE DYNAMICS OF MOBILE APP GROWTH

In the vast digital expanse where mobile apps reign supreme, growth is both an aspiration and a challenge. The dream of every developer is to see their application flourish, witnessing a surge in user engagement, downloads, and positive feedback. However, with this growth comes the crucial challenge of scalability—ensuring that the app's performance remains impeccable even as its user base expands exponentially.

The Importance of Scaling in the Mobile Ecosystem

The mobile ecosystem is unique. Unlike traditional software where upgrades or changes might be scheduled and controlled, mobile apps are constantly on the frontline. With millions of potential users accessing apps simultaneously from various devices and regions, ensuring an uninterrupted and seamless experience becomes paramount. This is where the importance of scaling becomes evident. Scaling doesn't merely pertain to handling increased user traffic; it encompasses optimizing databases, enhancing server capacities, refining user experiences, and often reimagining architectural strategies.

A Glimpse into the Stages of App Growth

Every app's growth journey can be visualized as a series of stages. Initially, during the launch phase, the focus is on market penetration, user acquisition, and establishing a foothold. As the app starts gaining traction, it transitions to the growth phase, characterized by rapid user acquisition and increased engagement. However, it's the subsequent scaling phase that truly tests an app's mettle. This phase demands infrastructural robustness, adaptability, and a proactive approach to potential challenges.

This guide, "Scaling and Managing Growth for Mobile Apps 101," is crafted to be your compass during this scaling journey. From understanding the initial indicators that signal the need for scaling to diving deep into infrastructural adjustments, cloud solutions, monitoring, security, and continuous deployment —every chapter is meticulously designed to offer insights, strategies, and best practices.

Whether you're a budding developer witnessing your first app's growth or a seasoned professional managing a portfolio of expanding applications, this guide aims to equip you with the knowledge and tools necessary to navigate the intricate dynamics of mobile app growth.

Prepare to embark on a journey of discovery, challenge, and immense learning. Let's scale new heights together!

CHAPTER 1:
RECOGNIZING THE
NEED TO SCALE

Growth is exhilarating. As more users begin to download and engage with your mobile application, it signals that your product is resonating with its target audience. However, beneath this surge lies a series of technical challenges that, if not addressed timely, can hinder the user experience and even jeopardize the app's reputation. Recognizing the signs that indicate a need for scaling is the first step in this intricate journey.

Indicators of Scalability Needs

Every app, regardless of its platform or purpose, will exhibit specific signs that scream 'time to scale.' Here are some of the most common indicators:

    1. Slow Response Times: As user interactions multiply,

you might notice a decline in the app's responsiveness. Functions that used to execute almost instantaneously now lag or hesitate.

2. Increased Load Times: Loading screens or pages taking longer than usual are clear indicators that the current infrastructure is struggling with the traffic.

3. Uptick in App Crashes: No user likes it when an app unexpectedly crashes. If the frequency of crashes goes up, it might be a sign of the system getting overwhelmed.

4. Database Strains: Challenges in retrieving or storing data, or even outright failures, point towards database scaling needs.

5. Negative User Feedback: User reviews can be invaluable. If you're receiving feedback about reduced app performance or delays, it's a direct cue from your audience to upscale the infrastructure.

Proactive vs. Reactive Scaling

There are two predominant approaches to scaling:

1. Proactive Scaling: This involves forecasting growth based on trends and scaling your infrastructure in anticipation of that growth. By analyzing metrics like monthly active users, session lengths, and user acquisition rates, developers can make educated estimations about future demands and adjust resources accordingly.

2. Reactive Scaling: In this approach, scaling actions are

triggered in response to specific events or thresholds. For instance, if server utilization consistently hits 90%, additional resources could be automatically deployed.

While reactive scaling is often more economical in the short term, it can sometimes result in momentary performance hiccups. Proactive scaling, though demanding a higher initial investment, ensures a consistently smooth user experience.

Understanding when and how to scale is a delicate balance of technical foresight, user feedback, and strategic planning. As we delve deeper into the subsequent chapters, we'll uncover the nuances of different scaling strategies, ensuring your app remains robust and efficient amidst rapid growth.

CHAPTER 2: INFRASTRUCTURE SCALING - VERTICAL VS. HORIZONTAL

As your mobile app continues to expand its user base, the underlying infrastructure needs to keep pace. But how should you approach this growth? There are two primary methods to scale the infrastructure supporting your application: vertical scaling (scaling up) and horizontal scaling (scaling out). Making the right choice depends on your app's needs, budget constraints, and long-term goals.

The Benefits and Limitations of Vertical Scaling

Vertical scaling, often referred to as "scaling up", involves enhancing the capacity of your current setup. This might mean upgrading your server's RAM, CPU, or storage.

Benefits:

1. Simplicity: Vertical scaling doesn't require significant changes to your existing architecture or application

code.

2. Reduced Complexity: Since you're working with a single server, there's no need to manage multiple systems or worry about distributed data.

Limitations:

1. Hardware Limits: There's a ceiling to how much you can upgrade a single server.
2. Downtime: Often, scaling up requires server downtime, which can affect user experience.
3. Cost: High-end servers can be expensive, and the price-performance ratio might not always be favorable.

Advantages of Horizontal Scaling and Distribution

Horizontal scaling, or "scaling out", involves adding more servers to your setup and distributing the load amongst them.

Advantages:

1. Flexibility: You can easily add or remove servers based on demand, making it a more elastic solution.
2. High Availability: If one server fails, others can take over, ensuring continuous availability.
3. Geographical Distribution: For global apps, servers can be distributed across regions, ensuring optimal performance for users worldwide.

Challenges:

1. Complexity: Managing multiple servers introduces complexities, especially concerning data consistency and synchronization.
2. Network Overhead: Data transfer between servers can introduce latency.

When deciding between vertical and horizontal scaling, it's essential to consider both the immediate needs and the long-term trajectory of the app. While vertical scaling might suffice for smaller, sudden spikes in user activity, horizontal scaling is generally more sustainable for consistent, long-term growth.

In the chapters ahead, we'll delve into the intricacies of optimizing app architecture, embracing cloud solutions, and other advanced techniques that work hand-in-hand with these scaling strategies, ensuring that as your app grows, it remains swift, reliable, and efficient.

CHAPTER 3: OPTIMIZING APP ARCHITECTURE FOR SCALABILITY

As the user base of a mobile application expands, mere infrastructure adjustments might not be sufficient. The architecture—the very backbone of your app—often demands a reevaluation and optimization to ensure continued seamless performance. This chapter dives into critical architectural considerations and modifications to enhance scalability.

Stateless Design Principles for Scalable Apps

At the core of scalable architectures lies the principle of statelessness. A stateless application doesn't save client data generated in one session for its use in the next session with that client. Instead, each session is treated as a new interaction.

Advantages:

1. Flexibility in Request Handling: Any server can handle any request since no server retains session-specific data.
2. Reduced Memory Usage: Not storing session data means less memory consumption, leading to efficient resource utilization.

Considerations:

1. Session Management: For apps requiring session data, external systems like Redis or databases can be used to manage and store session information.
2. Increased Database Calls: Since session data isn't stored in the application, it might lead to increased database queries.

Database Optimization Techniques

The database is often the heart of any application. As the app scales, ensuring that the database can handle the increased demand becomes crucial.

Techniques:

1. Database Indexing: Creating indexes on tables can drastically speed up data retrieval times.
2. Denormalization: Sometimes, introducing redundancy by denormalizing tables can enhance performance by reducing join operations.

3. Sharding: Distributing the data across multiple servers or databases can ensure that no single server becomes a bottleneck.
4. Caching: Using caching mechanisms like Memcached or Redis to store frequently accessed data can reduce database calls and enhance speed.

Challenges:

1. Data Consistency: With techniques like sharding or caching, ensuring data consistency can become a challenge.
2. Backup and Recovery: More complex database setups might require intricate backup and recovery solutions.

A truly scalable mobile app is underpinned by an architecture that is both robust and adaptable. The strategies above, when implemented judiciously, can ensure that as your user base grows, your app remains resilient, responsive, and reliable. As we navigate through subsequent chapters, we'll delve into the synergistic aspects of cloud solutions, monitoring, and other facets that tie into and complement a scalable architecture.

CHAPTER 4: CLOUD SOLUTIONS FOR APP GROWTH

The cloud has revolutionized how applications scale. With the power to dynamically allocate resources, adapt to traffic spikes, and offer global accessibility, cloud platforms have become a cornerstone for scalable mobile app architectures. This chapter delves into how cloud solutions can bolster app growth and ensure consistent performance.

Embracing Cloud Platforms for Flexible Scaling

The traditional approach of managing and maintaining physical servers comes with constraints—both in terms of cost and scalability. Cloud platforms, on the other hand, offer vast, flexible resources on-demand, allowing apps to scale as needed without major upfront investments.

Benefits:

1. Dynamic Resource Allocation: Cloud platforms can automatically assign more resources during high traffic and scale down during lulls, ensuring cost-effectiveness.
2. Global Reach: With data centers worldwide, cloud platforms ensure that your app offers consistent performance to users across the globe.
3. Maintenance and Updates: Cloud providers handle server maintenance, security patches, and hardware upgrades, allowing developers to focus solely on the application.

Auto-Scaling and Global Distribution Features

One of the cloud's standout features is its ability to auto-scale. Based on predefined metrics (like CPU usage or incoming traffic), the cloud platform can automatically provision or de-provision resources.

Advantages:

1. Cost Efficiency: You pay for what you use. During

off-peak hours, the resource usage (and cost) can be significantly reduced.

2. Performance Stability: During unexpected traffic surges, auto-scaling ensures the app doesn't crash due to resource constraints.

Global Distribution:

1. Content Delivery Networks (CDN): Cloud platforms often integrate with CDNs, distributing app content across a network of servers worldwide. This ensures users access data from a server near their location, enhancing speed.
2. Geo-Replication: Some cloud platforms allow databases to be replicated in different geographic regions, ensuring data availability even if one region faces outages.

While cloud platforms offer immense benefits, it's essential to choose a platform aligned with the app's needs. Whether it's AWS, Google Cloud, Azure, or any other provider, each brings its unique features and pricing structures.

In the following chapters, we'll continue our journey through app scaling by exploring monitoring tools, understanding the role of CDNs in depth, and examining how to ensure data integrity and security in a rapidly scaling environment.

CHAPTER 5: MONITORING, ANALYTICS, AND UNDERSTANDING USER BEHAVIOR

To successfully scale an application, developers must have a clear, real-time understanding of its performance, potential bottlenecks, and the behavior of its users. Monitoring and analytics tools offer these insights, enabling proactive responses to emerging issues and strategic decisions based on user interactions.

Essential Tools for Performance Monitoring

Performance monitoring tools provide a comprehensive view of how an application is functioning. They track various metrics like server health, response times, error rates, and more.

Key Tools:

1. New Relic: A comprehensive application performance management tool that offers insights into app performance, error tracking, and user interactions.
2. Datadog: Provides cloud-scale monitoring, allowing visualization of performance metrics, traces, and logs in one integrated platform.
3. AppDynamics: Tailored for large enterprises, it monitors application performance and offers root cause analysis for issues.

Benefits:

1. Proactive Problem Identification: Before users notice an issue, monitoring tools can highlight performance dips or error spikes, allowing swift corrective actions.
2. Optimization Insights: Regular monitoring can identify potential areas for optimization, like reducing load times or enhancing database queries.

Analyzing User Patterns for Proactive Scaling

Understanding how users interact with an app is crucial for scaling. Analytics tools can provide insights into user behavior, highlighting features that are popular, paths taken within the app, and times of peak activity.

Popular Tools:

1. Google Analytics for Mobile: Offers insights into user demographics, behavior, and app performance.
2. Mixpanel: Focuses on user interactions within the app, helping identify popular features and potential pain

points.

3. Amplitude: Provides product analytics to help teams build better user experiences.

Benefits:

1. User-Centric Scaling: By understanding user behavior, resources can be allocated to support popular features effectively.
2. Feature Development: Analytics can guide the development roadmap, emphasizing features users love or improving areas they avoid.

In the realm of scaling, knowledge is power. By continuously monitoring performance and understanding user behavior, developers can make informed, strategic decisions, ensuring the app not only scales effectively but also resonates with its growing audience. As we delve deeper into subsequent chapters, we'll explore advanced scalability tools like CDNs and the complexities of balancing load across distributed systems.

CHAPTER 6: THE ROLE OF CONTENT DELIVERY NETWORKS (CDNS)

In a digitally connected world, ensuring that users from every corner of the globe experience consistent app performance is a substantial challenge. Content Delivery Networks, or CDNs, emerge as a powerful solution, optimizing the delivery of app content based on user location. This chapter delves into the significance of CDNs in scaling mobile apps and ensuring uniform, swift content delivery.

Introduction to CDNs and Their Benefits

A Content Delivery Network is a system of strategically positioned servers that work together to deliver content (like images, videos, stylesheets, JavaScript, and more) to users based on their geographical location. Instead of every user request going to the primary server, it gets redirected to the nearest CDN server, ensuring faster content delivery.

Key Benefits:

1. Speed: CDNs reduce the physical distance between the user and the server, decreasing the time taken to fetch content.
2. Reduced Load on Origin Server: By handling numerous user requests, CDNs reduce the load on the primary server, enhancing its performance and longevity.
3. Uptime and Availability: With multiple servers distributed globally, even if a few servers face issues, others can take over, ensuring uninterrupted content delivery.
4. Protection against DDoS Attacks: CDNs can identify and counteract malicious traffic, shielding the primary server from potential DDoS attacks.

Implementing CDNs for Mobile App Growth

Adopting a CDN isn't just about choosing a provider and integrating it. It requires careful planning to maximize its potential.

Strategies:

1. Content Prioritization: Determine which content pieces are frequently accessed and ensure they're cached in the CDN for quicker delivery.
2. Cache Control: Set appropriate cache durations for different content types. Dynamic content might have shorter cache durations, while static content can remain

cached longer.

3. Geographical Analysis: Analyze where the bulk of your users are located and ensure that the CDN servers in those regions are optimally utilized.

Popular CDN Providers:

1. Akamai: One of the pioneers in the CDN realm, Akamai boasts a vast network and offers advanced security features.
2. Cloudflare: Beyond content delivery, Cloudflare provides a range of security features, including protection against DDoS attacks.
3. Amazon CloudFront: Integrated with AWS services, CloudFront offers a reliable, scalable CDN solution with a pay-as-you-go pricing model.

In the journey of app scaling, CDNs play a pivotal role, bridging the gap between growing global user bases and consistent app performance. As we venture into the subsequent chapters, we'll explore further intricacies of scalability, like managing loads across distributed systems and ensuring data integrity amidst rapid growth.

CHAPTER 7: LOAD BALANCING AND DISTRIBUTED SYSTEMS

As your mobile application grows, ensuring that every user request is processed efficiently becomes paramount. The traffic influx can strain a single server, leading to slower response times or even system crashes. Enter load balancing and distributed systems—strategies designed to distribute incoming traffic, ensuring smooth performance even during peak loads.

The Mechanics of Load Balancing in Scalable Systems

Load balancing refers to the process of distributing incoming network traffic across multiple servers. By doing so, no single server is overwhelmed, resulting in faster response times and high availability.

Key Components:

1. Load Balancer: A device or software that acts as a reverse proxy, directing client requests to the most appropriate server.
2. Server Pool: A group of servers where the traffic is directed, with each server capable of delivering the application.

Benefits:

1. Redundancy and Reliability: If one server fails, the load balancer redirects traffic to the remaining online servers.
2. Efficiency: Servers are used optimally, ensuring efficient use of resources.
3. Flexibility: New servers can be added or removed from the pool easily, providing adaptability as traffic demands change.

Exploring Modern Distributed System Architectures

A distributed system is a collection of independent computers that appear to users as a single coherent system. In the context of mobile apps, distributed architectures help scale out applications, ensuring they remain resilient and scalable.

Advantages:

1. Scalability: Systems can be expanded by adding more

machines to the network.

2. Fault Tolerance: Even if a subset of servers fails, the system continues to operate.
3. Resource Sharing: Resources such as storage or processing power can be shared across the network.

Challenges:

1. Network Latency: Communication between servers can introduce delays.
2. Data Consistency: Ensuring consistent data across multiple servers becomes a challenge, especially in real-time applications.
3. Complexity: Managing and maintaining a distributed system can be complex, requiring specialized tools and expertise.

Popular Solutions:

1. Kubernetes: An open-source platform designed to automate deploying, scaling, and operating application containers.
2. Apache Mesos: A distributed systems kernel that abstracts CPU, memory, and storage away from machines, enabling fault-tolerant and elastic distributed systems.
3. Docker Swarm: A native clustering and scheduling tool for Docker containers.

Effective load balancing and adept use of distributed systems are integral to the scalability journey. They ensure that as user numbers swell, the application remains steadfast, responsive, and efficient. As we delve deeper into subsequent chapters, the focus will shift towards data integrity, security, and other vital facets of app scaling in a complex digital landscape.

CHAPTER 8: ENSURING DATA INTEGRITY AND SECURITY DURING SCALING

In the throes of scaling a mobile application, while the emphasis often lies on performance, uptime, and user experience, there's another crucial aspect that cannot be overlooked—data integrity and security. As the infrastructure evolves and becomes more complex, safeguarding user data and ensuring its consistency becomes paramount.

Addressing Data Consistency Challenges

Distributed systems, while excellent for scalability, introduce challenges in data consistency. With multiple servers handling requests, ensuring that every server has the latest, most accurate data is crucial.

Strategies:

1. Database Replication: By creating copies of databases, you ensure data availability. However, care must be taken to synchronize these replicas to prevent data discrepancies.
2. Atomic Transactions: Ensure that database transactions are atomic, meaning they're either fully completed or fully rolled back, preventing partial updates.
3. Consensus Protocols: Algorithms like Paxos or Raft ensure that operations in a distributed system are executed in order, ensuring data consistency.

Security Protocols for Growing Mobile Apps

As your app scales, it becomes a bigger target for malicious entities. Implementing robust security measures is non-negotiable.

Key Measures:

1. Encryption: Use encryption both in transit (TLS) and at rest (disk encryption) to ensure data confidentiality.
2. Regular Security Audits: Periodically review and assess the app's security posture. Identify vulnerabilities and rectify them.
3. DDoS Protection: Use services like Cloudflare or AWS Shield to mitigate Distributed Denial of Service attacks.

4. Authentication and Authorization: Implement strong authentication mechanisms and ensure users can only access data they're permitted to.
5. Backup and Recovery: Regularly back up data to recover from potential breaches or data loss incidents.

Tools and Solutions:

1. OAuth: A widely-adopted protocol for authorization, especially useful for token-based authentication.
2. JWT (JSON Web Tokens): A compact, URL-safe means of representing claims to be transferred between two parties.
3. Let's Encrypt: A free, automated, open Certificate Authority that can be used to generate SSL certificates for encrypted connections.

Protecting user data and maintaining its integrity is not just a technical requirement but also a trust factor. Users trust applications with their data, and it's the responsibility of developers and businesses to uphold that trust. As the journey of this guide continues, we'll explore the advanced terrains of continuous integration, deployment, and understanding the intricate tapestry of modern, scalable mobile applications.

CHAPTER 9: CONTINUOUS INTEGRATION AND CONTINUOUS DEPLOYMENT (CI/CD)

In a rapidly evolving digital landscape, the ability to quickly and efficiently roll out new features, improvements, and patches is invaluable. However, with a growing user base and a more complex infrastructure, this process needs to be seamless, ensuring that updates don't disrupt user experience. This is where Continuous Integration and Continuous Deployment (CI/CD) come into play.

Streamlining Development with CI Pipelines

Continuous Integration (CI) is the practice of merging developers' changes into a main code branch frequently, sometimes multiple times a day. This continuous merging allows teams to detect and fix integration errors early.

Key Components:

1. Version Control Systems (VCS): Tools like Git provide a platform where multiple developers can collaborate without overriding each other's changes.
2. Automated Testing: Every code change goes through a series of automated tests, ensuring that new additions don't introduce bugs.
3. Feedback Loops: Developers receive immediate feedback on their changes, allowing for quick corrections.

Best Practices in CD for Scaling Apps

Continuous Deployment (CD) takes CI a step further. Once the changes pass through the CI pipeline, they're automatically deployed to the production environment.

Advantages:

1. Rapid Releases: New features or fixes can be delivered to users quickly.
2. Reduced Manual Errors: Automated deployment processes reduce the chances of human errors during deployment.
3. Optimized Resource Utilization: By automating deployment, resources are used more efficiently, freeing up teams to focus on development.

Implementation Strategies:

1. Feature Toggles: Instead of withholding code changes until they're complete, deploy them hidden behind a

"toggle". This allows teams to test new features in a live environment without affecting users.

2. Canary Releases: Deploy new changes to a small subset of users. Monitor performance and feedback, and then roll out the change more broadly.
3. Blue-Green Deployment: Maintain two production environments (Blue and Green). One hosts the live version (Blue), while the other (Green) is used for new releases. Once tested, traffic is switched to Green, making it the new live version.

Popular CI/CD Tools:

1. Jenkins: An open-source tool offering a vast plugin library, making it highly customizable for CI/CD.
2. Travis CI: A cloud-based CI service that's seamlessly integrated with GitHub repositories.
3. GitLab CI/CD: A comprehensive tool with capabilities for CI, CD, and more, integrated within the GitLab ecosystem.

Incorporating CI/CD into the app development lifecycle ensures that the application remains agile, adaptive, and consistently aligned with user needs. As we wrap up this guide, the concluding chapters will provide a holistic view of the scaling journey, emphasizing the importance of iterative improvement and proactive adaptation in a dynamic mobile ecosystem.

CHAPTER 10: EMBRACING A CULTURE OF CONTINUOUS IMPROVEMENT

In the context of mobile app scaling, the technological adjustments, strategies, and optimizations are only one part of the equation. The other crucial element is the mindset with which these changes are approached. Embracing a culture of continuous improvement is foundational to navigating the challenges of scaling and ensuring sustained success.

The Growth Mindset in Mobile App Development

A growth mindset, as opposed to a fixed mindset, is characterized by the belief that abilities and intelligence can be developed through dedication and hard work. For app developers, this translates into continuously seeking improvements, being receptive to feedback, and viewing challenges as opportunities.

Key Aspects:

1. Iterative Development: Instead of viewing app development as a linear process, see it as cyclical —design, develop, test, release, gather feedback, and refine.
2. Feedback Loops: Encourage user feedback and implement mechanisms to actively gather it. Feedback is the compass that guides improvement.
3. Lifelong Learning: The digital realm is ever-evolving. Regularly update skills, explore emerging technologies, and stay updated with industry best practices.

Adaptive Strategies for Ever-Changing User Demands

User preferences, behaviors, and needs aren't static. As technology evolves, so do user expectations. An adaptive strategy is one that's flexible, responsive, and proactive.

Components:

1. User-Centric Development: Always prioritize user needs. Regularly conduct user experience (UX) tests and ensure the app aligns with user preferences.
2. Agile Methodologies: Embrace agile development processes that prioritize flexibility, collaboration, and

customer feedback.

3. Proactive Monitoring: Don't wait for issues to arise. Use monitoring tools to preemptively identify potential problems and address them.

Staying Ahead in a Competitive Landscape

The mobile app market is saturated and fiercely competitive. Continuous improvement ensures not just survival, but also differentiation.

Strategies:

1. Innovation: Regularly introduce new features or improvements that enhance user value.
2. Market Analysis: Stay updated with market trends, competitor moves, and emerging technologies.
3. Community Building: Foster a community around your app. Engaged users often provide valuable insights and are the best brand ambassadors.

In conclusion, while the technical nuances of scaling are undeniably important, the mindset and culture with which these challenges are approached are equally pivotal. A culture of continuous improvement, driven by user-centric development, proactive adaptation, and a thirst for learning, is the bedrock on which successful, scalable mobile apps are built.

CONCLUSION: THE HOLISTIC JOURNEY OF MOBILE APP SCALING

Scaling a mobile application is akin to navigating an expansive, ever-changing landscape. It's a journey marked by exhilarating highs of user growth, challenging terrains of technical complexities, and moments of reflection and recalibration. But at its core, scaling isn't just about expanding infrastructure or optimizing code—it's about ensuring that as the app grows, it continues to resonate with users, offering them value, efficiency, and delight.

Throughout this guide, we've journeyed through the intricacies of recognizing the need to scale, making infrastructural choices, optimizing architectures, embracing the cloud, monitoring performance, safeguarding data, and imbibing a culture of continuous improvement. Each chapter, each strategy, is a testament to the multifaceted nature of scalability.

A few key takeaways as we wrap up:

1. User First: At every juncture, prioritize the user. Whether it's refining features, ensuring uptime, or enhancing performance, the user's experience is the ultimate barometer of success.
2. Proactive Over Reactive: While reactive strategies have their place, being proactive—anticipating challenges and addressing them preemptively—can make the scaling journey smoother.
3. Continuous Learning: The digital domain is dynamic. Stay updated, be curious, and embrace the ethos of lifelong learning.

Lastly, remember that scaling is not a destination but a continuous journey. There will always be new horizons to explore, fresh challenges to tackle, and novel opportunities to seize. As you embark on or continue this journey, may this guide serve as a beacon, illuminating the path and ensuring that your app not only grows but thrives in the vast mobile ecosystem.

Thank you for joining us on this exploration. Here's to scaling new heights!

www.ingramcontent.com/pod-product-compliance
Lightning Source LLC
La Vergne TN
LVHW051752050326
832903LV00029B/2868